GUIDES

RETAILING

REAL LIFE GUIDES

Practical guides for practical people

In this increasingly sophisticated world the need for manually skilled people to build our homes, cut our hair, fix our boilers, and make our cars go is greater than ever. As things progress, so the level of training and competence required of our skilled manual workers increases.

In this new series of career guides from Trotman, we look in detail at what it takes to train for, get into, and be successful at a wide spectrum of practical careers. *Real Life Guides* aim to inform and inspire young people and adults alike by providing comprehensive yet hard-hitting and often blunt information about what it takes to succeed in these careers.

The other titles in the series are:

Real Life Guide: the Armed Forces

Real Life Guide: the Beauty Industry

Real Life Guide: Carpentry & Cabinet-Making

Real Life Guide: Catering

Real Life Guide: Construction

Real Life Guide: Electrician

Real Life Guide: Hairdressing

Real Life Guide: Plumbing

Real Life Guide: the Motor Industry

Real Life Guide: Working Outdoors

trotman

Real Life GUIDES

RETAILING

Dee Pilgrim

Real Life Guide to Retailing
This first edition published in 2004 by Trotman and Company Ltd
2 The Green, Richmond, Surrey TW9 1PL

© Trotman and Company Limited 2004

Editorial and Publishing Team
Author Dee Pilgrim
Editorial Mina Patria, Editorial Director; Rachel Lockhart,
Commissioning Editor; Anya Wilson, Editor;
Bianca Knights, Assistant Editor
Production Ken Ruskin, Head of Pre-press and Production
Sales and Marketing Deborah Jones, Head of Sales and
Marketing
Advertising Tom Lee, Commercial Director
Managing Director Toby Trotman

Design by XAB

British Library Cataloguing in Publications Data
A catalogue record for this book is available from the British
Library

ISBN 0 85660 999 4

Typeset by Photoprint, Torquay
Printed and bound in Great Britain by Cromwell Press,
Trowbridge, Wiltshire

Real
Life

GUIDES

CONTENTS

About the author

Dee Pilgrim studied journalism at the London College of Printing before working on a variety of music and women's titles. As a freelancer and a full-time member of staff she has written numerous articles and interviews for *Company, Cosmopolitan, New Woman, Woman's Journal* and *Weight Watchers* magazines. As a freelancer for Independent Magazines she concentrated on celebrity interviews and film, theatre and restaurant reviews for such titles as *Ms London, Girl About Town, LAM* and *Nine to Five* magazines, and in her capacity as a critic she has appeared on both radio and television. She is currently the film reviewer for *Now* magazine. When not attending film screenings she is active within the Critics' Circle, co-writes songs and is currently engaged in writing the narrative to an as yet unpublished trilogy of children's illustrated books.

Acknowledgements

Thank you to all the people who so kindly agreed to be interviewed for this book including Jamie Farquhar, Peter Dodd, Jonathan Baron and Sarah Welsh.

For his detailed analysis and comments on the retail industry many thanks to Peter McLaren-Kennedy of Skillsmart and also to Judith Meyrick of Skillsmart for her help on the training chapter.

Introduction

It's become something of a joke to talk about people who 'shop until they drop', but the retail business is anything but a joke. In fact, retailing – the process of selling goods to customers and all that this entails – is a very serious business that we all interact with every day of our lives. Just think about it for a moment: the clothes you are wearing have all been designed, manufactured and then bought from a retail outlet such as a boutique or department store; the food you eat came from a shop, most probably a supermarket; even this book you are reading could well have come from a W H Smith or a Waterstones. You will have local shops near to where you live, maybe a large supermarket in the area, and the high street of any town or city will be a bustling place with people intent on buying everything from TVs to bedding, while others will be just as keen to sell to them.

Over the last five years employment in retailing has grown by over 170,000 and with the UK economy still growing at a slow but steady rate the retail sector is bound to continue to grow.

Just how all encompassing the world of retail is becomes clear when you read the figures. In 2002 the total figure for UK retail sales was approximately £230.7 billion. That's an awful lot of bread, meat, apples, DVDs, pairs of jeans and mobile phones we've been buying. According to the Office of National Statistics, in 2003 the retail industry employed over 2.7 million people. That is a staggering 11 per cent of the total UK workforce, meaning one in every nine working people is in retail. Over the last five years employment in retailing has grown by over 170,000 and with the UK economy still growing at a slow but steady rate the retail sector is bound to continue to grow. In fact, vacancies for graduates have increased in retailing in the last few years while they have largely declined in other industries. However, you don't have to have a degree to get into this business as many companies offer training on the job and some have training schemes that even lead to National Vocational Qualifications (NVQs).

DID YOU KNOW?

The grocery market in the UK is now worth £75 billion a year.

Once upon a time a job in retail was not seen as either particularly exciting or sexy but that's certainly not the case now. With everybody wanting to buy, buy, buy, the opportunities to sell, sell, sell have broadened out massively. The growth of retail parks, American-style shopping malls and the huge increase in the mail order and Internet (e-tailing) markets means we can buy more things in more ways than ever before and so jobs within the retail trade are changing in order to reflect these trends. In fact, things change on the High Street (the industry's term for the major retail shops) so quickly you have to be a smart operator not to miss the boat. In recent years sales for such well-known names as Marks & Spencer, W H Smith and Sainsbury's have all suffered because they failed to spot customer trends, especially the burgeoning youth market, and when they did realise their mistakes they were too slow at correcting them. However, these are all established companies and probably won't disappear, they will just have to keep an eye on the competition and stay one step ahead. This is why retailing is an exciting business to be in, it moves fast, it constantly changes and it challenges its employees to keep coming up with new ways to part consumers from their money.

We may only see the people on the shop floor but there are plenty of 'hidden' jobs in retailing. As consumers we may only interact with the cashiers or sales assistants but there are also buyers, managers, marketing teams and distributors who all ensure we get the products we want to buy at the right time and at the right price. For the purposes of this book we shall be concentrating on those closest to the core of the retail trade, those involved with the actual buying and selling, although related businesses are mentioned so you can make a more informed choice as to which area within the industry you would like to work.

It's also good to remember that retail is a relatively youthful industry, with young people entering at the bottom of the career ladder but quickly progressing to the top. Many get to be board members by the time they are 40 – some even get to own the whole company!

If you are considering a job in retailing then this book will help you to make up your mind. Not only will it explain what positions are actually available, but it will also describe what different people actually do within the industry. It will tell you what qualities and skills you will need to get on and what personality traits will hold you back. It will explain how you can train and where you can look to find that all-important first job. Finally, the case studies will demonstrate just how varied jobs within the industry can be. A future career in retailing isn't a hard sell because this is an industry with great things ahead of it and, just think, you could be a part of it.

KEY TERMS

Like most industries retailing has its own set of terms used for specific situations. Here is a list of the most commonly used retail jargon.

DID YOU KNOW?

Oxford Street is the busiest shopping street in Europe with over five million square feet of shopping space.

BUSINESS TO BUSINESS (B2B)
This means when one business sells to another.

BUSINESS TO CONSUMER (B2C)
This is what happens when you go into a shop and buy something.

BRICKS AND MORTAR BUSINESSES
Traditional businesses that actually have shops and salesrooms rather than carrying out their business electronically.

CLICKS AND MORTAR BUSINESSES
A business that sells its goods through a combination of traditional outlets and electronically (see below).

E-COMMERCE/E-TAILING
These are sales carried out electronically over the Internet as opposed to bricks and mortar sales.

1

PETER DODD

Case study 1

THE BUYER

When 35-year-old Peter left school at 16 he went straight into the retail business, working on the shop floor for sportswear company Cobra Sports. His training was very hands on, dealing with customers, getting involved with deliveries and stock, and liaising with the management and Head Office. He quickly worked his way through the company, moving from sales associate (assistant) to assistant manager, then manager and area manager when he became involved with trouble-shooting (including the hiring and firing of staff) for the firm's West End store. After ten years he felt there was nowhere left for him to go so he moved sideways to the company's warehouse in Chiswick. This dealt with all the Cobra Sports stores in London and Peter was responsible for the logistical side of things, sorting out POS stock, the inventory and handling an awful lot of deliveries. After three years, Peter was made redundant just before the firm went bankrupt. He then worked for Talbots ladies' fashion retailer and Soletrader shoe stores before joining DKNY 15 months ago.

You really have to have a logical, no-nonsense, let's get the job done, hands-on attitude to do this job.

C-SHOPS

Once known as the humble corner shop, or local convenience store, this is now one of the biggest growth areas in retail. Both Tesco and Sainsbury's have tried to muscle in on this market with Tesco Metro and Sainsbury's Local stores, with the other big supermarket groups queuing up to buy job lots of c-shops. However, the big names are still Spar, Co-op and Londis.

THE HIGH STREET

Where once this term applied literally to the shops on your local high street it now applies to all the well-known larger retail chains that have a presence in our towns and cities including Sainsbury's, Tesco, Marks & Spencer, Next, Dixons and W H Smith.

POINT OF SALE (POS)

This refers to the physical location at which goods are sold to customers, often a promotional display unit.

T-COMMERCE

Sales carried out through the television.

Mainly working out of the Donna Karan DKNY store in London's Bond Street, Peter is now a buyer/stock controller for the company.

'I basically just got fed up with the shop floor side of retail – always having to work at weekends and on late-night shopping evenings. That really got me down and also, if I'm honest, I had lost interest in selling, it didn't offer me a challenge any more. Now I am really involved with the buying side for DKNY. I liaise with New York (where the company originated) every day mainly by telephone or fax and that means getting into the office as early as 7am or 8am because of the time difference. I like to iron out any problems before the shop in Bond Street actually opens. I am part of a team of buyers and my responsibility is buying the fabrics we use to make our clothes.

DID YOU KNOW?

Tesco's Cherokee and Florence & Fred clothing labels are the fastest growing clothing brands on the High Street.

'There's a company called Premier Vision in France and they bring over new fabrics twice a year and I frequently visit them as well. I also visit our warehouse in Holland where I oversee the quality control. I go and see the people, organise what we are buying and what costings we have budget-wise and once the material comes to us here I then organise its redistribution to Portugal and to the Philippines where our garments are made. I also have to liaise with the management team and our visual team and work out what is selling where, so if something is selling well in Cheshire and not in London I will organise the redistribution of the surplus stock. I also organise promotions, like this week we had a PURE event to

promote our pure cotton and pure linen ranges and I
organised the production of freshly prepared smoothies in
our in-store bar.

'You really have to have a logical, no-nonsense, let's get the
job done, hands-on attitude to do what you do. The things I
like most about working here are the regular Monday to
Friday hours, the fact the money is very good and the team
is great. I also get to travel for my job – apart from France
and Holland I have also visited New York once or twice.
However, I see this (my job) as a bit of a stepping-stone and
I really want to progress here at DKNY in the next four or five
years. There is the possibility of being relocated State-side or
of becoming overall logistics co-ordinator for the company. I
would also really like to achieve more recognition within the
company. To go out on a high would be to source and to
buy in a fabric that becomes the talk of the season.
Something like the new Prince of Wales check!'

2

Buying power

If you have looked at the business pages of the major newspapers in the last few months, you may have gained the impression that all was doom and gloom within retail; profits down, sales figure forecasts down and the price of shares in many of the major retail companies falling. However, according to Peter McLaren-Kennedy, the head of communications at Skillsmart, the retail Sector Skills Council, this is really not the case at all. 'Overall, the industry is in good shape but there will always be winners and losers because we are at the sharp end here where the ups and downs are very quick and very noticeable. The reason for this is the industry has got so much more competitive. This is because consumers have less loyalty to brands now and will shift from one to another very quickly if they perceive they can get better value elsewhere.'

At present, the retail market is split into five main categories:

- food and drink
- fashion
- leisure and entertainment
- household
- online e-tailing.

However, as McLaren-Kennedy points out, things move quickly in the industry as a whole and there are some significant new trends appearing within these categories with many retailers actually blurring the lines between them. Below he points out the most significant trends that are affecting the way retailers sell and the way we buy.

LUXURY GOODS

'The luxury end of the market is booming, especially with regard to fashion items. This is because there is a small but significant group of people with very large amounts of money who are willing to spend it on quality. For basic goods, people tend to look for low prices, but for luxury items, especially designer clothes and furniture, they are willing to splash out.'

FOOD

'The opportunities for the big supermarkets have been limited by the fact many can no longer get planning permission to build out-of-town superstores and as they can only go so far in stealing custom from the competition they are looking to the corner shop (c-shop) market as a new format for them, taking over smaller, existing premises in or near the centres of cities and towns.

'The organic market is growing steadily but prices still make it out of the reach of great numbers of people. Meanwhile, ethical trading (spearheaded by the Fair Trade brand) is still a tiny niche market but certain companies such as the Co-op, Oxfam and Starbucks have all embraced it and they have pushed it up the agenda. However, the area of food that is really going to grow is away from foods that have high levels of salt, sugar and fat in them, foods that are bad for you. All the big food companies are developing recipes that are healthier. I know Marks & Spencer is launching a whole range of frozen foods with reduced amounts of salt in them. There is an onus on the companies to be responsible and offer their customers a healthier option and interestingly enough, there is now a real shortage of food technologists in this country, so jobs within that sphere are at a premium.'

SPECIALIST SHOPS

'One growing trend that is very interesting is new, specialist stores from names on the High Street we already know. For instance, Marks & Spencer now has 'Simply Food' and a dedicated furniture store in Gateshead. It has also opened stand-alone Per Una stores that stock and sell only its more trendy fashion Per Una brand. The John Lewis Partnership that owns Waitrose has launched two Food & Home stores (in London's Canary Wharf and Cheltenham) that are doing extremely well. Shopping has become a big leisure pastime because it is so much easier to shop with longer opening hours, Sunday opening and more disposable income to be spent, so expect more lifestyle-oriented stores.'

FASHION

'Younger, trendier fashion stores such as Zara and Mango have really made an impact on the market and are doing well at the expense of other established brands. I think we will see a lot more new brands coming in from Europe and America and we are bound to see a few mergers as well.'

DID YOU KNOW?

Maplin Electronics, the hi-tech retailer that currently has 83 stores, plans to open 13 new outlets in 2004. Pre-tax profits in 2003 rose by 40 per cent to £17.9 million with sales of sound and vision products up 36 per cent, hobbies and electronics up 23 per cent and computers up 33 per cent. The company was originally set up as a mail-order supplier by two telephone engineers working out of a bedroom in Essex.

Source: The Guardian

TECHNOLOGY BASED GOODS

'The technology based side is going to be huge, things like mobile phones, computers, personal music players like iPod, digital cameras and mini camcorders. Traditional retailers such as Dixons now have huge competition from the likes of Asda and Tesco and are really having to rethink their marketing which means this side of retailing is going to get very, very interesting.'

McLaren-Kennedy also thinks we will be using technology more to actually buy things with real growth in e-tailing and also between buying online and the storefront – an area where Tesco is in the forefront. He also believes we will see more companies using the Internet instore. All of this means the industry needs lots of new, enthusiastic employees to fill the new roles opening up and in the following chapter we explore just some of the jobs available if you decide to make a career in retailing.

The big sell

3

While many of us view buying things and even window shopping as a pretty fun thing to do, most of us would probably not have considered that a job selling can also be great fun and very rewarding. The world of retail never stands still and new technology means retailers are often the first to employ electronic tools such as scanners and computerised tills. But there is far more to retailing than just buying and selling and in this chapter we will explore just what it is different people within the retailing world actually do. As stated previously, this book deals mainly with the people closest to the core of retailing which includes those who work on the shop floor and also the managers, buyers, and display staff who work in and around the stores and also at Head Office. We will also be looking at associated careers such as marketing and distribution. The chart below gives you some idea of the variety of jobs you can do in the retail trade.

DID YOU KNOW?

Online retailer Amazon.com made its first annual profit in the tax year 2003/2004. For the full year the company reported a net profit of $35.3 million.

JOBS IN RETAIL

In the warehouse
DISTRIBUTORS
TRANSPORT STAFF
LOGISTICS CO-ORDINATOR

In the store
CHECKOUT STAFF
SALES ASSISTANT
PRODUCE ASSISTANT
RECEIVING SUPERVISOR (STOCKROOM STAFF)
VISUAL DISPLAY ASSISTANT
ASSISTANT MANAGER
DEPARTMENT SALES MANAGER
CUSTOMER SERVICE STAFF (CUSTOMER SERVICE
DESK)
PERSONAL SHOPPER

At head office
BUYER
HUMAN RESOURCES
PR (PUBLIC RELATIONS) DEPARTMENT
IT/TECHNICAL BACK UP
MARKETING
MERCHANDISING

In other locations
DESIGNERS
FOOD TECHNOLOGISTS
MANUFACTURERS/PRODUCERS
CALL CENTRE STAFF

Before looking at these jobs in greater detail, let's first explore what your work environment will be like – just where is it you will actually be working? The place where you spend your working life will depend on what you do in retail, but here are just some of the locations (with actual examples) you may find yourself in during your working hours.

POSITIONS WITHIN RETAILING

In a convenience or corner store **LONDIS**	Within an inner city shopping mall **MANCHESTER ARNDALE CENTRE**
In a medium-sized supermarket **TESCO**	In a call centre **FREEMAN'S**
In a department store (or concession stand within a department store) **DEBENHAMS**	On a ferry, a plane or a train (or in airports, ports and stations) **HEATHROW/ WATERLOO**
At Head Office **BOOTS**	Within a huge out-of-town retail park **BLUEWATER**

In an exclusive, luxury designer store **ARMANI**	In a DIY centre or in a garden centre **B&Q**
In a market **BOROUGH MARKET**	In a warehouse **IKEA**

IN AND AROUND THE SHOP FLOOR

SALES STAFF

Once perceived as rather low in the pecking order, good sales staff are actually vital to the success of any business. This is because they provide the human face of retailing. They are the bridge between the public and the company they work for and good, efficient, polite sales staff are more likely to make customers come back to your shop or store than individuals who are sullen, ill-informed and can't be bothered. Sales staff include sales assistants. These are the people who remain on the shop floor replenishing shelves or rails, returning unwanted goods to their correct sector, directing customers to specific areas of the shop, and helping to pack bags and take purchases to the customers' cars. They include retail cashiers and checkout operators whose job has been revolutionised by the advent of new technology. Where once their responsibility was simply to take payment for goods and provide the correct change, these days they may also be handing out cashback, dealing with credit cards, handling both Euros and pounds and also making sure customers are using their store loyalty cards.

CALL CENTRE OPERATIVES

In mail-order businesses, and to a lesser extent click and mortar businesses where there is no face-to-face contact between the customer and retailer, the role of call centre operative is very important. They are the voice, if not the face, of the company and when people ring in to place orders or to query a non-delivery, a payment or a price, the operative must be able to deal with the enquiry quickly and positively. They must be able to think on their feet and remain polite and patient at all times, even when the customer isn't right! Once again, if they do their job properly the company is more likely to get return business from its customers and a happy customer means more sales.

PRODUCE ASSISTANTS

In supermarkets and food stores generally (butchers, greengrocers, fishmongers) you will find produce assistants. They are responsible for making sure out-of-date items or damaged goods are removed from the shelves, that the display looks attractive to the customer and that everything is properly labelled and priced. They may have to move stock if there is a special offer on and check with stock control if certain goods are not coming down the supply line quickly enough. As with all members of the sales staff, they really have to have good knowledge of what the store actually stocks, what the product actually is and what it looks like. For instance, produce assistants in the greengrocery section are given specific training so they can recognise what all the different exotic fruit and vegetables such as okra and kumquats actually look like.

PERSONAL SHOPPER

As people's lives become increasingly stressed the role of personal shopper becomes more important. Many people are now cash-rich but time-poor, they simply cannot spend hours browsing through a store looking for their perfect purchases. This is where the personal shopper comes in. He or she is usually employed by a large department store and their job is to know the store's stock inside out. They build up a relationship with a customer, finding out their personal preferences, and then choose items they think are ideally suited to that customer. They could be looking for anything from a special outfit for a wedding to Christmas presents for members of their client's family. Personal shoppers must have exceptional social skills, be very discreet, and also be alert to new trends and fashions coming through.

CUSTOMER SERVICES

Another area where social skills are of paramount importance is in customer services. Customers have always had queries and complaints that customer services have had to sort out, but their role is now much bigger as stores have introduced new services to ensure customer loyalty. Now customer services can arrange a personal shopper for you, they can organise electric scooters and wheelchairs or other mobility vehicles for customers, they can also organise delivery to your door. In large department stores they can check the availability of certain items via their central computer system and track down that very last size 10 dress that just happens to be in their sister store in Aberdeen while the customer is in Bristol. They can even arrange for it to be transported to the customer's home store via their nationwide distribution service. Sorting out refunds, getting points added to customer loyalty cards, arranging financial services such as loans and exchanging faulty goods are all part of a day's work for customer services and so obviously, communication is of vital importance here. You also have to be able to stay calm under pressure and not lose your temper when things do go wrong.

DISPLAY STAFF

This is one of the more creative sides of the industry and as such it attracts a lot of people and so competition for jobs in display is quite healthy. Positions include visual display assistant, window dresser and display manager or (display) merchandiser. They take responsibility for all the in-store displays as well as the all-important window displays that attract the customers into the store in the first place. Displays have always been changed in conjunction with the arrival of the new season's goods so customers can get a taste of what is new around the store, and these days it is not unheard of for displays to be changed on a weekly basis, just to keep them one step ahead of the competition.

Display staff in the larger stores usually follow guidelines handed down from head office as to colours and themes, but must then use their imagination and creative talents to produce displays that really entice customers in. They will also be responsible for the upkeep and cleanliness of the displays. (One famous Christmas display for a large London store had the theme 'Cornucopia' and featured a fountain spraying red wine. Unfortunately, the heat of the lights caused the wine to ferment and foam, and so the display manager was forced to find a product that could be mixed with the wine and stop the foaming before the display was ruined.) Many experienced display staff leave full-time employment and prefer to work on a freelance basis.

BACK ROOM BOYS AND GIRLS

STOCK ROOM STAFF

The retail staff you don't normally see on the shop floor are just as important to the retail industry as their more visible counterparts. No large supermarket could exist without the shelf-stackers who replenish stocks, mainly while the stores are closed so they don't get in the way of shoppers. Then there are the stock room staff. They work behind the scenes unpacking deliveries, sorting them, pricing up certain items and ensuring they are ready to be taken out into the store. You need to be very precise to do this because you will be counting in deliveries and will have to chase up any discrepancies on delivery dockets and purchase orders.

RECEIVING SUPERVISOR/WAREHOUSE STAFF

The receiving supervisor acts as the bridge between the stock room staff and the staff in the warehouse where goods are stored before travelling to the stores and this part of the retail business is known as distribution (or supply chain). These days most of the retail supply chain is controlled electronically. As each item passes through the tills, the information on its colour and size stored within the barcode is passed on to the central stock control computer and replacement stock is ordered automatically. Smaller businesses may still do this manually by physically counting items of stock. Either way, the receiving supervisor still has an awful lot of paperwork to do, checking and crosschecking when new stock comes in. Many of the larger retailers own

DID YOU KNOW?

Small retailers account for 99.8 per cent of the retail industry.

their own warehouses; smaller retailers tend to use independent warehousing companies.

TRANSPORT STAFF

Finally, the transport staff or delivery staff are those that actually drive the lorries between the warehouses and the stores and they also tend to offload the goods from their vehicles and wheel them into the stores. These days they may also be driving the vans that deliver food orders placed via the Internet (such as Waitrose's Ocado service) direct to customers' homes.

WHOLESALE

Bear in mind that in wholesale (where one business sells to another business that will eventually sell to the consumer, i.e. a wholesale fashion house that will buy product in bulk and then sell on smaller amounts to a variety of independent fashion shops or boutiques) many of the roles within retail are replicated. For example, most wholesalers will employ sales staff, stockroom staff, warehouse staff, design staff and distribution staff.

DID YOU KNOW?

In Spring 2004, the Chief Executive of Boots announced plans to invest £390 million to modernise its 1,400-store chain to fight back against supermarkets stealing its traditional trade.

HEAD OFFICE/MANAGEMENT

BUYERS

If you think buying stuff for a living sounds like a dream come true, think again. Although the role of buyer is perceived as glamorous and high profile, it is also essential, high pressure and hectic. To a certain extent the buyer has to second-guess what people will want to buy in the coming months. They evaluate products that are already available and decide which they think will sell best in their stores. They also have to negotiate the best possible price with their suppliers (keeping in mind how much they think their customers will be willing to pay for them. Get this wrong and it can seriously affect profit margins).

If the precise product the buyer wants is not available he or she may order something to be made uniquely for their market and must ensure both the product quality and price. Most buyers specialise in one product area, e.g. ladies' or men's fashion, accessories or home furnishings and they need to have specialist knowledge of their market with an eye on fashions, fads and trends. Because of this they will work closely with the merchandising department, however much of their work will be out of the Head Office, actually talking to suppliers and there are good opportunities for travel in this role. Many people get into buying by first becoming buyer's clerks who assist the buyers by processing orders, talking with the suppliers and handling samples. (See 'Case Study 1'.)

DESIGNERS

Think about most of the goods you buy and you will soon realise the importance of the designer's role. From shoes to clothes, fridges, chairs and patterned fabrics, a designer has been involved in the evolution of that product. Designers must always keep one step ahead of fashions, predicting what people will want to buy in the future. They also have to be practical about what they are designing (they use the term ergonomics – is what they are designing suitable for its intended role? The bottom line is does it work efficiently?). Most designers study to higher education level and have a degree in design. It is a demanding job but can also be incredibly creative and rewarding.

FOOD TECHNOLOGIST/TECHNICIAN

As previously stated, the food technologist is now in high demand as the major food retailers are constantly looking to upgrade recipes and introduce new recipes to entice customers to buy. The company briefs the technologist or technician on what they are specifically looking for (i.e. low fat, low salt foods) and then he or she must create a recipe from scratch, constantly testing it and refining it until the desired flavour/consistency/texture/look is attained.

MERCHANDISING

If you can predict a fashion trend (the 'goth' look is going to be big next Christmas or chiffon scarves are making a massive comeback) then a job in a merchandising department may be just the thing for you. One of the retailer's biggest nightmares is being left with loads of stock nobody wants – that fluorescent green teddy bear for Easter, chocolate truffle stuffing for Christmas. When major retailers get their merchandising forecasts wrong it can have a disastrous affect on sales and profits (this has recently happened to Marks & Spencer). However, get it right and stock will be flying out of the stores faster than you can restock it. This makes merchandising an exciting place to be but you have to have a good analytical mind to make it in this department because you will be scouring statistics about the market and predicting what is hot and what is not.

MARKETING/PR

The merchandiser will rely on information from the marketing department to help them make informed decisions about products. That's because the people in marketing will be out there, talking to customers and looking at press coverage to see what it is people actually want to buy. They gather their information through the media and by conducting customer questionnaires. They are also responsible for promoting the products wherever they can, increasing customer awareness. They are responsible for marketing campaigns such as special offer vouchers and advertising in the local and national press.

Similarly, PR or public relations is responsible for raising customer awareness of your brands or product. PR departments can be in-house (i.e. based at Head Office) or independent and the PR will answer any queries or requests from members of the press. They will arrange samples to be sent out for magazine shoots, send out press releases containing new product information, inform the press about upcoming promotional events such as photo opportunities with celebrities and generally keep their company's name in the spotlight. Communication skills and being a real people's person are essential to work in PR.

IT/TECHNOLOGY
If technology and computers are more your bag then the IT department could be the place for you. If you want to get ahead in retailing you have to have computer skills. You will be dealing with complicated computerised tills on the shop floor; in the stock room information about the amount of stock coming in and going out is now computerised and nearly every major store worth its salt has its own website. Just think about it, even five years ago almost no one ordered their food over the web, but nowadays it is commonplace to see minivans from Tesco and Sainsbury's

driving up to people's homes and delivering their groceries straight to their front doors. These orders have been placed over the web and it is up to the IT departments to constantly update websites and ensure new systems are in place and running efficiently.

HUMAN RESOURCES

Retail is a cut-throat industry and everyone wants the best people to come and work for them. Also, once they have got the staff they desire, they want to hang on to them for as long as possible. The amount of talent poaching that goes on in the higher echelons of retailing is unbelievable, but keeping hold of staff further down the ladder is just as important. This is because training takes time and money and you don't want to lose one well-trained member of staff only to have to start the process from scratch with someone else. The human resources department (HR) is there to make sure employees are happy and working to their full potential. HR will organise recruitment and training. It will nurture employees' career development plans and talk through any problems such as personality clashes. It will also handle pay and benefits, and oversee (if necessary) any disciplinary procedures.

MANAGEMENT

The further you go up the retail promotional ladder the more responsibility you will have and those that ultimately have the most responsibility are the managers. You will be overseeing not only the stock and the staff but also the stores themselves and their profit margins. You need to be committed, concentrated and keen and the managers who show the most enthusiasm can quickly rise from the lowest levels to the highest. Most start as management trainees, learning the ropes while actually doing the job. Trainees often move around from department to department or different job areas of a business so they can get a good grounding in everything. From here they usually progress to assistant manager, where they have more responsibility but ultimately report to a manager above them.

Within large stores you can become a department sales manager where you are responsible for a specific department such as ladies' fashion, or maybe the electrical department. If you are working for a company with a large number of stores dotted around the country you could become a regional manager where you could have as many as 20 stores in your jurisdiction. You don't need to be a graduate to make it into management in retail, how far you get depends more on your own unique talents and abilities, and it is nice to bear in mind that some people who started out on the shop floor have made it all the way up to managing director. This shows the possibilities for advancement in retail really are as far reaching as you want to make them. (See 'Case Study 2'.)

E-COMMERCE POSITIONS

Many of the jobs mentioned above are replicated within e-commerce companies. They may not need sales assistants on the shopfloor but they will need sales staff to process customers' orders, customer care employees to deal with queries and complaints, managers, and human resource staff. However, the most important and biggest area of employment within e-commerce is in IT. For a start the company's website has to be designed and maintained and this will need the services of IT consultants, software support staff and hardware engineers. They may also employ a systems analyst or developer. If you are interested in the world of e-commerce you will need excellent computer skills and bear in mind that most of the vacancies in the IT area are at graduate level. For more information on jobs within this sector, have a look at *E-Commerce Uncovered*, published by Trotman.

DID YOU KNOW?

Asda's clothing label — George — is now a £1 billion brand making it the fifth biggest clothes retailer in the UK.

OTHER AREAS

Other areas in retail you might like to consider are becoming a security guard (most large stores now employ their own security operatives), owning/managing your own shop (everything from a patisserie to a boutique) or being a market trader with your own market stall.

By now you should have a better idea of the jobs you can do in retail, but what do you want to do – and more importantly, what are you actually suited to doing? In the following chapter we will be exploring the talents and abilities that will help you get on in some positions and the character traits and physical aspects that may make you unsuitable for others.

4

JAMIE FARQUHAR

Case study 2

THE STORE MANAGER

As a youngster Jamie was a big fan of tennis, starting to coach other people by the age of 16 and by 17 he had his tennis coaching qualifications. His love of tennis has now spilled over into his working life as he was recently made the store manager of the Pro Shop selling tennis racquets, sports shoes and sportswear at Chelsea's exclusive Harbour Club, which has the biggest indoor tennis club in London. Jamie studied a BA Honours degree in Leisure Management and Sports' Studies before joining the Harbour Club as a receptionist. While in this post he became aware that the Pro Shop within the club was looking for a sales assistant and he applied and got the job. Within three months he had been given a pay rise and after four months he became the acting manager and officially became the manager after five months when the exiting manager left and the assistant manager went off on maternity leave. His duties include serving customers, checking the emails from buyers, checking the stockroom and keeping it in order, sending back faulty stock, scanning deliveries, and doing the stock check every Monday. At

I take pride in making sure people are getting the right tennis racque or shoes for them. It's all about doing the best thing for the customer.

the age of 23 Jamie is now responsible for three other staff (one full-time, two part-timers) and a shop with an annual turnover of £475,000. His ultimate aim is to become the manager or owner of a tennis club.

'It was weird (when I became manager) because one Monday I walked into the shop and I was the most senior person there and I was suddenly in charge. The first two weeks were difficult because I had to learn so much and now I know nearly everything I need to know. Now the buck stops with me if anything goes wrong.

I have to sort out their wages, do all the banking and I have to send off the monthly sales figures to Head Office. I have to make sure the staff are motivated and busy and happy and I have to do their job reviews.

'I'm in charge of the three other staff and responsible for their training – everything from stock discrepancy knowledge, through sales to how to deal with faulty goods. I have to sort out their wages, do all the banking and I have to send off the monthly sales figures to Head Office. I have to make sure the staff are motivated and busy and happy and I have to do their job reviews. I'm constantly in touch with our buyers and I get reps in to show new product to myself and the staff because it is great training as they give us such detailed information about their products.

'The great things about the job are that we sometimes get freebies from reps and I love the fact we are so busy all of the time, although it can be tiring by Friday. However, it goes so quickly I don't have time to worry about stupid things, the only thing I can think about is my job, which is brilliant. I'm really involved in it all and I love making the shop look nice and I love helping the customers. I take pride in making sure people are getting the right tennis racquet or shoes for them. It's all about doing the best thing for the customer.

DID YOU KNOW?

Green & Black, the ethical, organic chocolate company, is expected to make sales of £14 million in 2004 with sales in 2005 expected to grow by about 40 per cent.

'The downside is that it does get stressful because there is a hell of a lot to do. That's why I'm trying to teach the other members of staff all I can so they know as much as possible and can help me.

'To get on in retail I think you have to work hard and have discipline. I also think you should get as much experience as you possibly can. Get a Saturday job while you are still at school working as a sales assistant. Get involved, get stuck in and learn as much as you possibly can.

'There are 25 Pro Shops around the country and I could now become manager at one of our bigger branches such as the one in Teddington. However, I am so happy at the moment working where I do I don't really want to move. Now, with my experience I think I'm getting equipped to achieving my dream of managing a tennis club. If I can do the job I am doing here I can definitely manage a club.'

5

Suits you, sir

Now you will have a better idea of what it is people actually do in retail, but is it for you? This is a business where things move very fast and constantly change so if you like a quiet life you may wish to explore jobs which are less demanding. However, if you have a real passion for retail, like the bustle and the rush you get from meeting new people and doing different things every day, then you could be one of the young, dynamic employees the industry is crying out for.

Remember, in retail you can move up the promotion ladder extremely quickly, which means pay rises and more professional kudos, but you must be really hungry for success in order to get it.

Remember, in retail you can move up the promotion ladder extremely quickly, which means pay rises and more professional kudos, but as anyone already in the industry will tell you, you must be really hungry for success in order to get it. In chapter 11, 'Career Opportunities', we will explore just how you go about getting into the industry, but here we list the personal qualities, attributes and strengths you can bring to the job that will give you a head start over rival candidates. The world of retailing doesn't suit everyone, but this list will help you to make up your mind whether or not you suit it and it suits you.

BEING A PEOPLE PERSON

If you are afraid to say boo to a goose you really should steer clear of retailing because if you can't talk to people and really communicate with them how are you ever going to sell them anything? In retail you are interfacing with people on a daily basis, some of whom you will know, while others will be total strangers. If you are on the shop floor you will be dealing with customers, if you are a buyer you will be talking to suppliers and if you are a manager you will be talking to staff, customers, buyers, Head Office and everyone else involved in the supply chain.

GOOD COMMUNICATION SKILLS

These lead straight on from being a people person. It's OK to smile and be friendly and polite, but if no one can understand what you are on about then you are not going to get very far. Whoever it is you talk to during the working day you must ensure they get the gist of what you are saying quickly and easily so that mistakes don't get made. This is of equal importance if you are talking on the phone or face to face, however if you work in a call centre it becomes even more important. Customers don't have the time to repeat everything they tell you down the phone so if they order a pair of jeans in size 12, long length, they expect you to take the order correctly and for you to give them information on payment and delivery clearly and efficiently. Remember, it's good to talk so make sure your communication skills are excellent.

BE ORGANISED

Customers expect good service when they are out spending their hard-earned cash and if they come across a shop that runs smoothly and gives them what they want hassle-free they will be more inclined to stay loyal to it. This is why you need to be organised. You want the whole selling and buying process to run smoothly. Being organised includes being a good timekeeper, making sure you have clean uniforms if you wear one, keeping good records if you are involved in stocktakes and remembering to bring in name badges, keys to the stockroom and the other paraphernalia associated with your job. Having the basics of your working life sorted clearly in your mind will give you breathing space to deal with any problems that are bound to occur during the course of a busy day.

NUMERICAL SKILLS

Going hand in hand with the organisation of your everyday life is your ability to organise numbers. There are numbers everywhere in retail – from prices and price codes, to giving change and refunds, to stock lists and inventories – so if maths is Martian to you, you may find retailing just as alien. Even in the merchandising department you will be analysing statistics, looking at sales figures and getting stuck in with numbers, while buyers will have to decide just how much of a certain product to order. If sums do your head in then retail is really going to give you a headache.

FIT FOR THE JOB

Talking of headaches, there are some areas of retail where having good physical health will really stand you in good stead. If you work in the stockroom, warehouse or on the shop floor it is more than likely you will spend a significant part of your working life on your feet and you'll probably be doing a lot of walking. If you are a stockman or a sales assistant you may also find yourself doing a lot of lifting as you unpack new stock, move it around and/or put it out on display. You need to have stamina and strength. Many women sales assistants swear by support tights to help with tired, aching legs after a day on the shopfloor!

If you work in the stockroom, warehouse or on the shop floor it is more than likely you will spend a lot of your working life on your feet and you'll probably be doing a lot of walking.

BE DECISIVE

As a customer there is nothing worse than going into a store and asking an assistant a question, only for them to look back at you like a startled rabbit and say 'oh, I don't know!' This is not the right answer or the right attitude. You need to be decisive, i.e. make decisions quickly. The correct reply would be more along the lines of 'let me take you to the customer services desk/manager, they will be able to help you straight away!' It would, of course, be even better if you could answer the question yourself, but there are always going to be queries you haven't come across before, however dithering really isn't an option – make the decision to find out. If your managers can see you are capable of making the right decisions under pressure they are more likely to put you forward for promotion.

ABILITY TO COPE WITH STRESS

So how stressful can selling a few apples be anyway? The answer is 'very'. Retail moves so fast the demands on you will come as a constant flow. Customers will need your help, Head Office may be crying out for sales figures, at Christmas product can move out of the store so fast you have to fight to keep shelves and rails stocked. What happens if the automatic doors to the store get jammed shut, or a till goes offline, or a delivery van breaks down? You will have to learn to cope with the stress of working under pressure nearly every day. Having many of the qualities listed above will lower your stress levels simply because they will help you overcome the problems you encounter, but being able to stay calm and think straight are really going to help.

BE ENTHUSIASTIC
Whatever else you bring to a job in retailing, enthusiasm will take you the farthest. An eager, smiling employee, willing and able to tackle anything his or her manager throws at them will soon become an invaluable member of staff. Being enthusiastic will really help you progress quickly because so much of what you learn in retailing is learnt on the job. If you take on all the jobs you can you will gain experience across a whole range of retailing positions.

LOVE THE PRODUCT
One of the best bits of advice for anyone coming into the industry is to know what you like yourself as a consumer. If you are fanatical about music, working in a music store such as HMV is going to suit you more than working at B&Q. If you are a fashion junkie then apply for jobs with fashion houses or boutiques. If beauty products press your buttons then what about working for a beauty franchise such as Clinique in a department store or starting out at a chemist or drugstore. You become a better salesperson when you love what you sell and have a deep knowledge of it because customers pick up on your passion.

THINGS TO CONSIDER

All the above are positive attributes you can bring to a job in retailing, however there are several things you should take into consideration that may put you off before you even begin.

ANTISOCIAL HOURS

Many jobs in retail require that you work at weekends and do some late evenings a week. In some areas people will also work overnight (doing big stock takes or restocking the store). It is also more than likely your store will be open on Bank Holidays and over Christmas. If you are not prepared to work antisocial hours you may have to rethink a career in retail.

PHYSICAL DISABILITIES

If you suffer from a physical disability that makes getting around difficult there may be jobs in retail that won't suit you. However, many of the bigger retailers such as Marks & Spencer actively encourage those with disabilities through special schemes to pinpoint the most suitable positions.

SHYNESS

You can't be a shrinking violet in retail or as quiet as a mouse – you have to get out there and interact with your work colleagues and with the public – so if being around other people and talking to them all day long gives you the shivers, you'd better think of another career.

LOW PAY

It's likely your wages will not be very high when you start — this can change quickly as you move up the retail ladder, however if you are not prepared to put up with low pay when you initially start work in retail, especially if you are on the shop floor, you may like to consider doing something else.

BEING ON YOUR FEET

If you are working on the shop floor or in a warehouse then it is highly likely you will be on your feet for much of the day. You will probably be doing a lot of walking too – getting stock from the stockroom, finding items for customers and returning unwanted stock from the changing rooms. If your idea of the perfect job is sitting behind a desk all day then all this standing and walking probably means a job in retail is not for you.

RETAIL QUIZ

If you still think a career in retail could be for you then the following section is a fun way to see just how much you really know about the industry. Based on things that happen around the shop floor it will test your knowledge of customer care and retail awareness; do you really know what a sales assistant's responsibilities are and if you did join a retail company would you be a profitable resource? Simply choose the answer you believe is right or is closest to what your own response to a situation would be. And don't worry if you get some wrong, making sure you know the right answers is why all these companies have training schemes!

1. Someone comes into your c-shop and brings a bottle of wine and some beers up to the cash desk. In what circumstances would you be within your rights to refuse to sell it to them?

A. Because you believe them to be under 18 years of age and they do not have any ID on them proving their age?

B. Because you think they are already under the influence of alcohol?

C. Because you are not 18 yourself yet?

2. Which of the following is the most important reason a store could give for poor sales figures over the Christmas period?

A. Christmas stock arrived in the store too late to take advantage of the whole Christmas buying period?

B. Stock was displayed at the wrong places within the store so customers weren't aware of it?

C. The stock was priced too high so customers were put off buying it?

3. At the till a customer pays for some goods with a cheque. However, when you compare the signature on the cheque guarantee card with the one on the cheque you become suspicious because they don't seem to match. Do you:

A. Shrug your shoulders and accept the cheque anyway; it's not your problem if the signature is a forgery?

B. Ask for further proof of the person's signature, such as a Visa card or store card?

C. Simply refuse to let the customer buy the goods?

4. You see a customer take an item off a shelf and hide it under their coat. What should your first action be?

A. Alert the store security because they are obviously shoplifting?

B. Go up to the customer and ask them if they would like a basket, or if they would like help with their purchases?

C. Turn a blind eye?

5. What is the legal minimum age you can sell a customer a cutlery set that includes knives?

A. 16 years old?
B. 12 years old?
C. 18 years old?

6. While you are on the shop floor a customer approaches you with a query about the price of an item. You don't know the price off the top of your head and the item doesn't appear to have a price tag on it. Do you:

A. Direct the customer to the till saying they will handle it there?
B. Try and find another member of staff who might know the price?
C. Go with the customer to the till and check the price yourself?

7. A customer says she has seen a drop-dead skirt in a magazine and that it comes from your store. Unfortunately, your particular branch doesn't appear to stock it. What do you do?

A. Tell her you've sold out of that item?
B. Give her the number of Head Office to ring when she gets home?
C. Explain that although you don't have it in stock, another branch may well do and offer to go to the

customer services desk with her where you can ring
Head Office to see if the skirt can be ordered for her?

8. During a stock check you discover two pairs of shoes are
missing. You're pretty sure you checked the delivery from
the warehouse correctly, so which of the possible
explanations below could account for the discrepancy?

A. There has been an internal transfer to another store
and someone has not filled out the necessary
paperwork?
B. A member of staff has stolen them?
C. A customer has stolen them from the display?
D. They were faulty and have been sent back to the
manufacturer?

ANSWERS
1. A and C. Under the Licensing Act, 1964 it is illegal to sell
alcohol to anyone under the age of 18, it is also illegal for
you to sell it if you are less than 18 years old yourself
unless you get the authorisation of an older member of
staff. Strangely enough, this law also applies to liqueur
chocolates!

2. All three. Apparently, these are the three reasons
Sainsbury's had poor sales figures over the 2003
Christmas period. By the time seasonal stock turned up
in the store many people had already made their
Christmas purchases elsewhere, others simply could not
find the Christmas stock because it was not displayed
prominently enough or wasn't in the right place within the
store. There was also the question of price. Many
customers thought prices were too high and so decided

to shop in other stores where prices were perceived to be better value.

3. B. Although you can't accuse the customer straight to their face, you can ask to see further proof of their signature, explaining it is standard practice. If the customer refuses you can then ask for an alternative form of payment – either cash, or a credit card (which will, of course, have another example of a signature on it). If the customer still refuses it is time to call in your line manager or your store loss-prevention team.

4. B. It is always best to try and deter possible shoplifters rather than wait until they actually commit the crime and then try to catch them. By offering a basket or your assistance you are alerting the customer to the fact they are under scrutiny and you are also giving them a chance to turn away from the act and go and pay for the item legitimately. If they decline your advances you can then alert a member of security to the situation. You should never, ever turn a blind eye to theft because it affects your company's profits. This can lead to higher prices for customers and affects you directly because it can mean bonuses are cut.

5. A. It is illegal to sell knives or blades of any kind to people under the age of 16. This applies to anything from a Stanley knife to a cheese grater.

6. C. Customer service is all in retail and your aim is to be polite and friendly, but above all efficient, so don't pass

the buck – deal with the query yourself. By taking the customer to the till you are showing they are personally important to your business. Apparently, one satisfied customer will tell ten people how pleased they have been with your service – that's a lot of good press to generate among potential customers.

7. C. Once again, it is all about customer service. These days inter-store transfers – those between one store and another – are exceptionally easy to handle because most of the work is done via computer. Most Head Offices not only know exactly how much of a particular item they have in stock, but also in which colours and sizes and in which branches. Many stores now offer a service whereby they will endeavour to order an item and get it to the branch of the customer's choice within 48 hours. Make the customer happy – it's what you are there for.

8. All four. Losses are broken down into two categories: known loss, such as breakages and damaged or faulty stock and unknown loss such as internal or external theft. This is why stock checks are so important – you need to keep track of where your stock is going. It should, of course, be going out of the front doors paid for by customers. If it is disappearing without payment then it is costing your firm

money. As part of the sales team it is up to you to do everything you can to combat loss and protect profits and this means making sure you fill out return forms correctly, being accurate in your stocktakes and keeping an eye on what is happening on the shop floor.

Well done! By now you really should have a good idea of how far your knowledge of the retail business stretches. Now is the time to find out what joining this dynamic industry would mean to you in terms of opportunities to progress and earn a decent living.

6

JONATHAN BARON

Case study 3

THE RECRUITMENT CO-ORDINATOR

Jonathan started his working life at a recruitment agency specialising in finding people for the retail sector. One of the agency's clients was a chain of computer retailing shops and 29-year-old Jonathan then moved to this company to work in its human resources department. He is now responsible for co-ordinating all of the recruitment for the group including personnel for Head Office as well as the sales staff for the stores.

'What I look out for in potential staff is resilience and ambition. Our staff need to be money driven, self-motivated and customer focused. The retail staff work on a commission basis so even though the basic wage is low when they first start, they can make it up as the commission is excellent.

What I love about what I do and about retail overall is the fact you are facing new challenges every day and there are targets you are aiming for.

What I look out for in potential staff is resilience and ambition. Our staff need to be money driven, self-motivated and customer focused.

'Most of our training is done on the job but we also have a training suite at Head Office where all retail staff go through an induction and where they can be brought in for retraining. Once trained the opportunities for progression are really good. Normally in our company people go from being a sales advisor to senior sales advisor and then to assistant manager, store manager, area manager and then Head-Office-based managerial positions.

'What I love about what I do and about retail overall is the fact you are facing new challenges every day and there are targets you are aiming for. Reaching them gives you great job satisfaction. Retail can be a job for life, either just on the shop floor selling, or as a long-term career progression up the retail ladder. The computer industry is an ever-growing market and so it is a very healthy area of retail to be in.'

DID YOU KNOW?

In 2002 the government brought in a supermarket code of practice to protect food suppliers against the might of the big retailers. As many people believe this has been ineffective the Office of Fair Trading (OFT) now plans to conduct a focused compliance audit of the four biggest retailers.

7

Making your mind up

You should have a really good sense of what retailing is all about by now, but deciding on the course of your future career is an important and difficult task. You may feel you have the qualities to make a go of it, but what of the wider retailing picture? Does the service industry sector have a bright future and what is in it for you? In what ways could working in retail enhance and improve your life? Below are listed some of the most common questions people joining the retail industry ask. Read the answers carefully because they will really help you to make up your mind if a career in retailing is for you.

ONCE QUALIFIED, CAN I MOVE UP THE PROMOTION LADDER QUITE QUICKLY?

You most certainly can. Take a look at 'Case Study 2', it will show how quickly you can progress from being a sales assistant to a sales manager. Also, as stated earlier, it is not unheard of for members of the board and managing directors to be in their late thirties and early forties. The big retail companies are very keen to keep hold of good staff, which is why they try and promote from within and so if you show a willingness to learn then the opportunities to progress are good.

WILL I BE ABLE TO MOVE INTO OTHER AREAS?

Certainly. Once you have achieved the required level of training and experience you could move sideways from sales into distribution or even across into buying (see 'Case Study 1'). In department stores there will be the opportunity to move between different areas (e.g. interiors, fashions, electrical goods) within the store. With big companies there may also be the possibility to relocate to different branches or to move from a branch or store to Head Office.

WHAT WILL MY TYPICAL HOURS BE?

As in most other service industries, there are no typical hours. Retail outlets need to be open to accommodate the needs of all their customers and this typically means at weekends and at least one late night a week (usually Thursdays) as well as 9am to 5pm (or 8am to 6pm) during most weekdays. Because of this, people who work in stores tend to do shift work, working a certain number of weekend hours and late night hours a month with time off in lieu. There is also the possibility of earning increased pay for working extra hours and antisocial hours including Bank Holidays. Jobs based at Head Office tend to entail ordinary office hours but even here, many employees work extra hours (buyers will be out and about talking to suppliers which may include travelling abroad). This can make a job in retail tiring, but the hours you put in will definitely pay off in the long run.

WILL I GET TIME OFF FOR HOLIDAYS?

Yes, you will, but they may not be when you traditionally take them! For instance, the Christmas period and annual January and summer sales periods are always frantic for the retail trade, so it will be all hands on deck at these times. Average holiday entitlement is between four and five weeks a year depending on whether you work full-time or part-time and who you work for. Bear in mind that many part-time staff are parents (single or otherwise) and may want to take time off during the school holidays, including half-term.

HOW MUCH CAN I EXPECT TO EARN?

The honest answer is not much to start off with, but with more training come regular pay rises. For instance, the most junior positions pay around £6,000+ per annum, while those entering junior trainee management can earn between £9,000 and £13,000. If you have a degree then your starting salary will be higher still. For instance, a new entry graduate into a buying position earns between £12,500 and £17,000 and after three or four years can be earning as much as £20,000. However, very experienced buyers and designers can earn £50,000. You may also get other benefits such as getting your uniform (if you wear one) free of charge, enjoying the benefits of staff discounts (these can be considerable) and a subsidised canteen and, with larger firms, the opportunities to join the company's pension or healthcare schemes. None of these should be sniffed at as they all help boost your financial status. Check out the leading retail recruitment websites to see what jobs and salaries are out there (see 'Resources').

WILL I BE ABLE TO USE MY SKILLS ABROAD?

Many people working in retail already do. Many buyers spend time in other countries sourcing new raw materials and/or products for sale into the UK market. Many companies in the UK are actually owned by foreign companies (ASDA is owned by American giant Wal-Mart) or are foreign themselves (Mango hails from Spain) and so British management may find themselves on fact-finding missions to Head Offices abroad. Some people, such as those who work in the shops on board cruise liners are, in effect, travelling as they are working. UK citizens have the right to work in any of the other European Union countries and if you are aged between 18 and 28 you can join the Young Workers Exchange Programme. This allows you to get some vocational training or work experience in another EU country for a period of time between three weeks and 16 months. Obviously, if you are travelling to countries where English is not the first language it really does help to speak the local language, and if working abroad is your goal then consider doing French, Spanish, German or other foreign language GCSEs.

Nowadays the industry has modern, well-trained staff who know what they are doing and can offer the customer real service, which has greatly improved the public's perception of the industry.

WHAT CAN I EXPECT TO GET OUT OF THE INDUSTRY PERSONALLY?

A real buzz of energy and excitement. At busy times you will be rushing around so much you won't know where the hours go. You will be at the cutting edge of the industry, seeing the new trends and innovations in fashion and interior design coming through the shop before members of the public ever do. You will have the opportunity to meet a really broad range of people from many different walks of life and some of them may even become your best friends. Just think, if you have a real love of the specific area you work in (food, electrical goods, beauty products) you'll be surrounded by it and involved in it every day of your working life. This is a young, dynamic industry where things vary from day to day as new stock comes in and seasonal changes are made, so you certainly won't have the time to get bored. But most importantly, you never need to get stuck in a rut in retailing because the opportunities to keep on training and moving up are open to everyone.

HOW WILL THE WIDER PUBLIC PERCEIVE ME?

Once upon a time people working in retail did not have a very respected image. According to Peter McLaren-Kennedy of Skillsmart this was because the industry was not good at training and retaining the best people and so turned out ill-prepared, unmotivated staff who did not offer the consumer a very good service. Nowadays the industry has got its act together, it has had to due to the cut-throat nature of the competition, and modern well-trained staff who know what they are doing and can offer the customer real service have greatly improved the public's perception of the industry. Although we haven't yet got to the American 'have a nice day' mentality of retail and other service staff, these days it is the norm to see smart, polite, smiling staff in our shops and stores.

EVENTUALLY, COULD I BE MY OWN BOSS?

You most certainly could. Just think of this staggering statistic: small retailers make up

DID YOU KNOW?

The Co-op doesn't just consist of retail units, it is also a bank, an insurance company, a travel company and has a string of funeral parlours. It now has an income of £8.1 billion.

99.8 per cent of the retail industry in the UK. These are the local family butchers on the high street, the little fashion boutiques and gift shops, the independent convenience store at the top of your road and the hardware stores, electrical shops, pottery and glassware and paper shops we all make use of but probably take for granted each and every day of our lives. Setting up on your own may seem like a scary prospect but according to McLaren-Kennedy, it doesn't even take huge amounts of investment to start your own store. What it does take is experience and a real knowledge of the industry, plus luck, flair and a talent for sniffing out what is going to be the next big thing. 'It is all about communication, attitude and creativity,' says McLaren-Kennedy. 'It's not reliant on you having a degree, it is about you as a person.'

Training day

8

The previous chapters should have given you a pretty good idea of whether a career in retailing is for you or not. If you are certain that it is, the next thing you will have to consider is how you enter the industry. Because retailing is such a dynamic and quickly expanding work sector, there are now many ways in which you can get industry-recognised qualifications. These can make your progression easier and faster, and if you are serious about getting to the top of the profession they will definitely help you achieve your goal.

There are two main routes for getting into the industry and you should think about them both carefully before choosing the route that is right for you. Because so much of retailing entails being hands on, one of the best routes is to get a job or become a trainee. By doing so you learn your skills at the cutting edge, and you can gain qualifications at the same time as earning a wage. These could be National Vocational Qualifications or Scottish Vocational Qualifications (NVQs/SVQs), or 'bite-size' or 'target awards' offered by awarding bodies. Such qualifications can be achieved on a part-time college course, through your employer or by undertaking Apprenticeships.

Apprenticeship programmes are usually run by the employer, or by an organisation in conjunction with the employer to provide both training on the job, which is supervised by a specialist, and training off the job on the employer's premises, at a college or training centre (either day or block release, or one or two evenings a week). The length of the programme varies from a few months to about two years. Many of the larger firms, such as Marks & Spencer, Tesco and Selfridges run their own industry-recognised training programmes, giving you the chance to earn as you learn. The employer benefits because new staff are getting trained to its own specifications, making it much easier to recruit and promote from within the organisation. The benefits to you are the fact you are actually employed and earning wages, and the qualifications you attain improve your career prospects and your job security. The training offered by such companies is also recognised and valued by other retailers.

Alternatively, you could take a full-time college course. Most full-time courses last one or two years and consist of a number of modules that cover different aspects of the job. Courses can lead to a BTEC First, National Certificate/Diploma and HNC/HND qualifications. BTEC courses include First Diploma in Retail and BTEC Higher National Certificate & Diploma in Retail Management. Some universities and colleges also offer Honours degree courses in retailing and related subjects. In fact, retailing is one of the UK's largest sources of graduate vacancies. A graduate training scheme normally lasts between one and three years. A new development is the introduction of Foundation degrees (FDs). These are employment-related higher education qualifications set at one level below an honours degree. FDs can be taken either part-time or full-time and are offered through universities and colleges.

Buyers usually enter the industry by becoming a buyer's assistant or buyer's clerk or via the degree, BTEC award or HND route. Once in a job most buyers are advised to gain professional qualifications via the Chartered Institute of Purchasing and Supply (CIPS) mainly because it is becoming increasingly difficult to progress without these or equivalent qualifications. CIPS schemes include block release, full-time and distance learning courses. (See 'Resources' for more information.)

Work-related industry-recognised qualifications are retail NVQs/SVQs, where you are assessed on a continuous basis and which are awarded at three different levels. There are NVQs/SVQs in Distributive Operations and Retailing Operations. How long it takes you to complete each level will depend on how quickly you complete each unit of work.

- Level 1 is an introduction to the job and ensures you have the basic skills.

- Level 2 is for more skilled workers who already know the basics. With this level you can enter the retailing industry as a retail assistant.

- Level 3 is for workers with greater responsibilities who will generally be first line managers supervising other staff or who have particular product knowledge and expertise.

Higher level NVQs/SVQs are available in more generic areas. Level 4 is for those who wish to take on more demanding management roles such as department heads.

There are two main levels to the Apprenticeship programme.

- Apprenticeship (FMA in Wales or Skillseekers in Scotland). This is based on the NVQ or SVQ Level 2 and because you are working at the same time as learning it usually takes about 12 months to complete. The Apprenticeship also includes Key Skills in Communication and Number as well as a vocationally relevant qualification.

- Advanced Apprenticeship (AMA in Wales or MA in Scotland). An Advanced Apprenticeship is based on NVQ or SVQ Level 3 and normally takes between 15 months and two years to complete. In Scotland the MA also includes five Core Skills and in England and Wales the Adavanced Apprenticeship includes Key Skills and a vocationally relevant qualification.

Apprenticeships are really aimed at school leavers and young people between the ages of 16 and 24. You could be eligible for funding providing you start your apprenticeship by the age of 25.

Further information on who to contact for these courses is contained in the 'Resources' chapter.

Although it is not essential to have paper qualifications to enter the industry, you will need some qualifications to get on to certain courses. For example, whatever further education route you decide to take, having GCSEs or Scottish Highers in English and Maths will come in very useful. Bear in mind some college courses do require a minimum of four GCSE passes and higher education institutions generally require two or three A-levels or Advanced Highers.

Getting good grades isn't the only thing you can do while still at school that will improve your chances of getting on in the industry. By far the best thing you can do is to get some experience actually working in a retailing environment. Arrange a Saturday or holiday job with a local store. Working part-time in retailing you will quickly acquire skills and knowledge to deal with customers and will get a taste of what really goes on and have the opportunity to watch what the trained members of staff actually do. This will really help you to decide if this is the career for you and if you decide to take a vocational route, such as an Appreticeship into the industry, prospective employers will be interested to see it included on your personal development plan (PDP).

In February 2004, Marks & Spencer launched Marks & Start, its new community programme. This gives work experience opportunities to everyone, no matter what their age or walk of life. With 2,500 places open each year the aim is to give people a real taste of what it is like to work in retail with

Getting good grades isn't the only thing you can do while still at school that will improve your chances of getting on in the industry. By far the best thing you can do is to get some experience actually working in a retailing environment.

placements lasting either two or four weeks. This will run alongside the existing Marks & Spencer's school work experience programme which gives young people between the ages of 14 and 16 the chance to do one or two weeks' work experience. These details were correct at the time of going to press but changes may be made so for more information call 020 7268 4502 (see 'Resources' chapter for the Marks & Spencer student support programme for talented individuals who are the first in their family to aim for higher education).

As anyone who ever turns on the TV these days knows, retailing is big business, from showing people 'what not to wear' to what to buy to make your home and garden more attractive. There are numerous magazines and books out there covering most sectors of retailing. Show your interest by either buying magazines or borrowing books from the library. Keep up with the latest clothing and home fashions by watching those shows on TV. Also read the local papers as they will have news stories on new stores/shopping malls opening in your area and you will be able to find out if they have any trainee places available by contacting them direct or by talking to your careers teacher or advisor.

> **DID YOU KNOW?**
>
> Boots was founded in Nottingham in 1877 and the group now includes Halfords and Boots Opticians.

Across the country, many colleges have become Centres of Vocational Excellence (CoVE) in specific subjects. For example, the London College of Communication is the CoVE for the retailing industry in London. You should ask your careers teacher or officer if there is a CoVE for retailing in your area. Alternatively, check out the www.dfes.gov.uk/cove website. You should also check to see what courses are actually available to you. As you will now realise there are numerous different options – ranging from courses for retail assistants to store management – so you need to know what is available and what you will be able to apply for. Once again, your careers teacher should be able to advise you, or check the websites of the main awarders of vocational qualifications that are contained in the 'Resources' section of this book to see what courses best suit your needs and abilities. Also, look at the websites of the well-known retailers – they provide lots of information on careers in their stores (see 'Resources').

BATTLE OF THE SUPERMARKETS

The supermarket sector is one of the most cut-throat in the whole of retailing with price-cutting wars, loyalty cards and new branding all trying to lure customers away from one store to another. In 2004 the market breakdown was:

TESCO	27%
ASDA	17%
SAINSBURY'S	16%
MORRISONS/SAFEWAY	15%

Opposite is an easy-to-follow guide summarising all the information contained in this chapter, from entry level right up to the most senior positions.

access to

NO QUALIFICATIONS

ENTRY LEVEL QUALIFICATIONS

FOUR GCSEs (A–D) grades 1–3
GNVQ/GSNVQ level 1
selection interview

ON-THE-JOB TRAINING

APPRENTICESHIP ✦ TRAINEE SCHEMES

ADVANCED MODERN APPRENTICESHIP (England)
SKILLSEEKERS (Scotland)
MODERN APPRENTICESHIP (NI)
MODERN APPRENTICESHIP (Wales)

Industry schemes e.g.
ASDA
SAINSBURYS
ARCADIA GROUP

e.g.
SHELF-STACKER
SALES ASSISTANT
WAREHOUSE STAFF
DRIVER
DRIVER'S MATE

CREDITS/FURTHER LEARNING

ON THE JOB QUALIFICATIONS ✦ PROFESSIONAL BODIES

NVQ/SNVQ
BTEC HNC/HND
Full-time/part-time/distance learning

Chartered Institute of Purchasing and Supply
(PICS)

CAREER OPPORTUNITIES

DEVELOPMENT OPTIONS

HIGHER EDUCATION ✦ MANAGEMENT ✦ OPEN OWN BUSINESS

9

SARAH WELSH

Case study 4

A DAY IN THE LIFE OF A SALES ASSISTANT
Single mum Sarah Welsh has worked part-time at the Hedge End out-of-town store Marks & Spencer for the last two years. This large, two storey building consists of a food department, homewear, menswear, children's department, ladieswear, lingerie, cosmetics, Autograph, Per Una and a Café Marks. Sarah works exclusively in ladieswear and her title is tilling and service assistant.

'I'm on the shop floor all of the time and I'm just constantly running around. I do a six-hour day from 9am to 3pm and the only time I sit down is my 15-minute break at 11 o'clock so I'm basically standing all day (we even stand when we are on the tills). On days when you do a four-hour shift you don't get a break at all.

'Our busiest times are Saturdays and Sundays of course, but also between 11am and 3pm when the children are at school. At 3pm it slacks off because people go off to do the school run. Other busy times are the sales and Christmas and last weekend we suddenly became manic in ladieswear because it was the

What I like best about the job is interacting with the customers and also the interaction with other members of staff, they're all great!

first nice sunny Saturday of the year and everyone was coming in to buy new, lightweight summer clothes.

'Last Saturday I did two two-hour stints on the till and I also did a stint in the ladies' fitting rooms. On another day I may also do some time on the customer service desk. There's not really a lot that can go wrong when you are on the tills because everything these days is computerised – it even tells you how much change to give. However, it is very rare for us to deal with cash or cheques, maybe only one transaction in ten will be cash while you might go a whole day and not see a cheque. Because of this at our store our till discrepancies are really low – something like one pence in every £100. The bulk of what we deal with on the tills is either credit cards or store cards, but mainly debit cards. At the moment I am being trained to be a till controller, that entails making sure people are at the right tills at the right time, that changeovers go smoothly, and dealing with any queries the till staff might have.

> **DID YOU KNOW?**
>
> The first quarter of 2004 saw sales figures in London much stronger than in Britain as a whole with retail sales up in Central London by 8.1 per cent on 2003. Apparently, sales were given a boost by Mothering Sunday where perfume, confectionary, stationery and home accessories performed extremely well.
>
> Source: London Retail Consortium (LRC)

'When we work in the fitting rooms we have to check the number of items in and the number of items out, put them on the rail and depending on how busy we are give assistance to customers who have queries. My main duties when I am on the customer service desk are dealing with returned items and customer orders because this is where people make the orders and also where they come to pick up orders once they have been delivered to the store.

'What I like best about the job is interacting with the customers and also the interaction with other members of staff, they're all great! The downsides are the antisocial hours (I work alternate Saturdays) and the fact we work very, very hard and it is incredibly tiring. At busy times we have as many as 39 people working in the ladieswear section alone. However, we do get other benefits. I get 20 per cent staff discount on goods and there is also a staff canteen where I'll go to have a sandwich and a drink on my break, and we have a wastage shop where we can buy discounted food when it is about to go out of date. We also get our uniform for free and I get a Christmas bonus, and there's a pension scheme that I am a part of.

'I'm happy with where I am at the moment but there are opportunities to move up to line manager and you also have the opportunity to transfer to other departments within the store if you want to. You need to have people skills to do what I do, you need to be polite and pleasant and be able to deal with people and it is ideal for single parents like me because of the flexibility of the hours I work.'

10

Career opportunities

If, by this stage of the book, you really have decided that retailing is for you, then the next course of action will be choosing what area of retail you want to enter, and also doing your utmost to make yourself the ideal candidate for the job.

Let's look at the different areas first.

- If you are **outgoing** and **sociable with good people skills**.

  These will all make you perfect as a member of the sales team. You will be talking to members of the public, answering their queries as well as serving them and generally interacting with others throughout your working day. Your social skills would also come in useful for talking to people on the phone as a call centre operative.

- If you like **travelling** around and **driving**, with a job where you visit various different locations during the day.

  A job driving a large delivery truck between the store and the warehouse, or driving a home delivery van between the warehouse or store and customers' houses would suit you. Bear in mind many drivers these days load and unload their own vehicles so you need to be quite physically healthy to do this job.

● If you like **making things**, are good at **art** and always looking out for new fashion trends.

Your interests and skills will make you ideal for joining a design department and eventually becoming a designer. The UK is becoming ever more design conscious and whether you design coffee cups or dresses, much of the retail trade is dependent on what concepts and designs your imagination can come up with. You would also make a good candidate for the visual display team where your creative talents could be used to increase sales.

● If you like working with **numbers** and are good at **mathematics** and anything involving logistics.

A job in the buying department, the accounts department or the merchandising department would suit you to a tee. In all three you will be dealing with sales figures, sales projections and statistics.

● If you are **patient** and understanding and like **solving problems**.

The customer services department is crying out for your skills. With diplomacy and tact you will be able to deal with everything from irate customers whose orders haven't arrived, to the new customer who wants to join your company's credit card scheme.

● If you like to be in charge, can handle a lot of **responsibility** and are **ambitious**.

You really should be heading into management. Here, the onus is on you to get things right and you will be responsible for those under your supervision. The stress related to management positions may be higher than in more lowly positions, but so too are the rewards. Once in management there are real opportunities to progress up the career ladder. Just think, you could eventually be managing director of the whole firm. Alternatively, you could decide to go it alone and become your own boss by opening your own store or shop.

HOW TO MAKE YOURSELF STAND OUT FROM THE CROWD

GET EXPERIENCE

Get yourself a Saturday job in a shop, be it on the counter of your local chemist or the till of a big superstore. Many large retail firms have their own work experience schemes (Marks & Start, etc.). This is by far and away the best method of discovering whether retail really is for you. Look out for job vacancies in the local press or apply personally to stores and shops.

HONE YOUR COMMUNICATION SKILLS

Talk to as many different people as you can. Don't just talk to people of your own age, but chat to older and younger people as well and it definitely helps to talk to people outside of your normal group of friends and family. In retail you will be talking to people from every different walk of life so the sooner you get used to communicating with them, the better.

KEEP YOUR SCHOOL GRADES UP

Although qualifications are not necessary for all jobs in retail, if you have a certain number of GCSEs it will definitely increase your chances of moving on quickly. On many college courses you will need four GCSE passes to be accepted, while in higher education the criteria is two or three A-levels or Scottish Highers.

BE INTERESTED

One of the best ways to show you are interested is to go out and window-shop: what does Mango have in stock at the moment? How does Dixons display its stock? What seasonal produce does Tesco have in store? Also, read mail-order catalogues (have a look through the Argos or Freeman's catalogues) and see what consumer trends are being talked about in magazines. If you've made up your mind what area of the trade you wish to join, then read the specialist publications concerning that area. These are widely available (see 'Resources').

BE ENTHUSIASTIC

No one expects you to know everything at the beginning of your career, but if you see each new challenge as something exciting that will further your promotional prospects rather than as something to be feared you will progress quickly. Be the first to put your hand up when managers are asking for volunteers, do tasks willingly and don't shirk work.

PAY ATTENTION TO YOUR PERSONAL APPEARANCE

Being smart and clean will make you a better prospective candidate for any job, but for those where you will be dealing with the public this is especially true. If you don't wear uniform make sure your clothing is appropriate for the store you work within (although you might get away with jeans and t-shirt in a record store, they may not go down so well in an upmarket clothes store). If you do wear uniform make sure it is clean and that you look tidy.

SMILE!
It's amazing how welcoming a smiling face can be. When you smile you are saying to people 'come and talk to me, I'll be able to help you'. You are also saying 'I'm a confident person' and people will be more willing to trust the judgement of a confident person, even if it is only as far as to tell them whether those shoes suit them or not!

LOVE RETAIL!
If you have decided this is really what you want to do with your life then learn to love the industry. This doesn't just apply to your own specific area but the whole of the retail trade. Every major newspaper has daily coverage of the trade within its Business pages. Here you will find out which stores are doing well, whose stock is going down, what the underlying trends are and also the future predictions. Make sure you read these pages. If you decide to move around within retail then these will give you the indicators you need to get jobs with the best companies and those with the brightest prospects.

> **DID YOU KNOW?**
>
> Forecasters predict that within the next five years c-shops and petrol forecourts will account for nearly £1 of every £3 spent on groceries.
>
> Source: Verdict

You can really fly high when you enter the world of retail. As you gain more experience and work your way up the career ladder you will discover what you like about it the most and will be able to make informed choices about where you eventually want to end up. The diagram below shows what you could be doing as you become better trained.

CAREER OPPORTUNITIES

BASIC TRAINING NVQ LEVEL 1

BASIC INTRODUCTORY SKILLS ✦ SALES ASSISTANT/SHELF-STACKER/
CHECKOUT OPERATIVE

MORE TRAINING
NVQ LEVELS 2 AND 3 (FMA/AMA)

MORE SKILLS AND EXPERIENCE ✦ FIRST LINE MANAGER/SUPERVISOR/
BUYER'S ASSISTANT

MORE TRAINING
NVQ LEVEL 4/HIGHER EDUCATION

DEPARTMENT MANAGER/BUYER/DESIGNER/HEAD OF MARKETING/
MANAGING DIRECTOR

11

The last word

By now you should be raring to set yourself loose on the fast-moving, ever-expanding retail industry. Having suffered a mini-recession at the beginning and middle of the 1990s when many high streets became ghost towns of closed stores, retail is booming again. It seems people's need to go out and buy is unstoppable and this means the need to find people to sell to them will continue to grow.

Now is a brilliant time to enter the industry because the retail sector as a whole is finally getting its act together and coming up with well-structured and well-defined training schemes that will give you the experience you need in order to succeed. Listed below are just some of the ways people in retail are training these days.

- Formal training courses – at colleges, either day release or evening release
- On-the-job training – with an external or internal training provider
- Buddying – where a senior member of staff becomes your buddy and shows you the ropes
- Seminars – where guest speakers from the industry will talk about certain aspects of it
- Workshops – where you usually deal with a specific subject, e.g. new technology
- Online, books and video learning.

A job in retail really can be for life and for those with the fire, drive and ambition it can be both financially and personally rewarding. As part of a successful team you will have the satisfaction of seeing your company grow and become more profitable. If you are on a bonus scheme you will feel the benefit of that profit in your own pocket and as you become more experienced you will be able to choose the job and the company for you. There are no shortages of job vacancies in retail (check out some of the recruitment websites in 'Resources') so this can be a very steady source of employment and how far you want to take it will very much depend on your own ambitions. Hopefully this book will have given you some indication of what retail is all about and what your role in this industry could be.

DO YOU LIKE MEETING LOTS OF NEW AND DIFFERENT PEOPLE?
☐ YES
☐ NO

DO YOU CONSIDER YOURSELF TO BE SENSIBLE AND RESPONSIBLE?
☐ YES
☐ NO

DO YOU HAVE GOOD COMMUNICATION SKILLS?
☐ YES
☐ NO

DO YOU HAVE DRIVE AND ENTHUSIASM?
☐ YES
☐ NO

ARE YOU A QUICK LEARNER?
☐ YES
☐ NO

ARE YOU A SELF-STARTER, ABLE TO TAKE CONTROL?
☐ YES
☐ NO

DO YOU LIKE FINDING OUT ABOUT NEW PRODUCTS?
☐ YES
☐ NO

If you answered 'YES' to all these questions then
CONGRATULATIONS! YOU'VE CHOSEN THE RIGHT CAREER!
If you answered 'NO' to any of these questions then this may not be the career for you.
However, you may like to consider some of the other careers mentioned here
such as warehouse assistant, stockroom staff or transport staff.

12

Resources

INDUSTRY BODIES

The British Retail Consortium
21 Dartmouth Street
London
SW1H 9BP
Tel: 020 7854 8900
Website: www.brc.og.uk

Skillsmart
Helpline:0800 093 5001
Website: www.skillsmart.com

The British Retail Consortium is the lead trade association for retailers from the big department stores right down to independents. You can find information on news, parliamentary issues and retail statistics on its website. However, if you want detailed information on courses and careers, you should contact Skillsmart.

This is the Sector Skills Council for the retail sector. Skillsmart has teamed up with learndirect to establish a retail-specific helpline that provides help, advice and guidance. It also produces a magazine called *Retail Therapy* full of news, case studies and advice. You should be able to get this from your school or your careers advisor, otherwise contact Skillsmart direct.

Chartered Institute of Purchasing and Supply
Easton House
Easton on the Hill
Stamford
Lincolnshire
PE9 3NZ
Tel: 01780 756777
Website: www.cips.org

CIPS is an international organisation serving the purchasing
and supply services. It currently has 17,000 members
worldwide studying for its qualifications. The start point for
qualifications is the CIPS certificate and advanced certificate
and you can go on to take the CIPS graduate diploma.
Detailed information on registration and qualifications is
contained on the website.

GOVERNMENT AND AWARDING BODIES

Connexions
Website: www.connexionscard.com

Connexions is aimed primarily at 13 to 19-year-olds and
gives excellent information on jobs and careers. In the
Career Zone section the Career Bank can offer you detailed
information on getting into retail as well as links to related
careers in the sector including food technician and fashion
designer.

Department for Education and Skills (DfES)
Packs available from 0800 585505
Website: www.dfes.gov.uk
Website: www.dfes.gov.uk/cove

If you are undertaking a vocational training course lasting up to two years (with up to one year's practical work experience if it is part of the course), you may be eligible for a Career Development Loan. These are available for full-time, part-time and distance learning courses and applicants can be employed, self-employed or unemployed.

City & Guilds
1 Giltspur Street
London
EC1A 9DD
Tel: 020 7294 2468
Website: www.city-and-guilds.co.uk

The leading provider of vocational qualifications in the UK, City And Guilds currently offers GNVQs and National Awards and National Diplomas in Retail as well as Retail and Distributive Services. Look at the excellent website where you can find exactly what is on offer under Retail and Distribution.

Edexcel
Stuart House
32 Russell Square
London
WC1B 5DN
Tel: 0870 240 9800
Website: www.edexcel.org.uk

Edexcel is now responsible for BTEC qualifications including BTEC First Diplomas and BTEC National Diplomas and Higher Nationals (HNC and HND). The website includes qualification quicklinks. BTEC qualifications in this field include Retail Management (vocational), Retail Operations (NVQ), Retailing (IVQ) and Visual Merchandising (NVQ). There have been recent changes to Edexcel so please check the website carefully.

Learndirect
Tel: 0800 100 900
Website: www.learndirect.co.uk

This free helpline and website can give you impartial information about learning.

Learning and Skills Council (LSC)
Modern Apprenticeship Helpline
Tel: 08000 150600
Website:www.lsc.gov.uk
Website: www.realworkrealpay.co.uk

Launched in 2001, Learning and Skills Council now has 48 branches across the country and is responsible for the largest investment in post-16 education and training in England. Its realworkrealpay website is specifically aimed at those who would like to do Modern Apprenticeships.

For MAs in Scotland you should look at:
www.modernapprenticeships.com or
www.careers.scotland.org.uk

For MAs in Wales you should look at
www.beskilled.net

INDUSTRY SCHEMES

Arcadia Group Ltd
Training Programmes Department
6th Floor
Colegrave House
70 Berners Street
London
W1T 3NL
Training Programmes Team: 020 7927 1112
Website: www.arcadiagroup.co.uk/recruitment

You may not know the name, but Arcadia is the largest
fashion retailer in the UK with over 25,000 employees. The
group includes such well-known brands as Burton, Dorothy
Perkins, Evans, Miss Selfridge, Topshop and Wallis. It has its
own Management Training Programme (MTP). It also has
entry-level positions in Distribution, Merchandising or Buying
as well as other vacancies.

ASDA
Website: www.asda.co.uk

For the past three years Asda has been in the Sunday Times
Top Ten companies to work for. The website gives
information on the Asda Graduate Scheme and also has
news of vacancies throughout its stores.

Marks & Spencer
Marks & Start
Tel: 020 7268 4502
Website: www.marksandspencer.com

Student Support
Website: www.marksandspencer.com/studentsupport

Marks & Spencer has a number of training programmes that you may be interested to join. For instance, its school work experience scheme offers 14 to 16-year-olds the opportunity to do one or two weeks' work experience with the company. This scheme comes under the umbrella Marks & Start scheme launched in February 2004. Apart from school children, placements will be given to those with disabilities, the young unemployed and those affected by homelessness. Another strand of the scheme is student support that is aimed at talented students who are the first in their family to go into higher education. Students are encouraged to go to university with Marks & Spencer providing financial support plus the opportunity to work in a Marks & Spencer store during the holidays and weekends to gain practical experience. This is aimed at students who wish to go into management.

Safeway
Website: www.safeway.com

Click onto Our Company and you will find information both on employment and careers within the Safeway group.

Sainsbury's
Website: www.sainsbury.co.uk

Once again, click onto Our Company and you will find sections on Jobs & Recruitment and vacancies including graduate vacancies.

Tesco
Website: www.tesco.com

Click onto Careers for information on job training and recruitment. Tesco is about to launch a brand new site for young school leavers but you can register here, at the existing site, to get information on Tesco's two training programmes including the Store Management Programme.

PUBLICATIONS AND PERIODICALS

The Appointment
PO Box 13145
London
N6 5QQ
Tel: 020 8340 3366
Website: www.theappointment.co.uk

This twice-monthly magazine focuses on news and developments in both the retail and leisure industries. Features include profiles of leading retailers.

Draper's (Record)
39 Bowling Green Lane
London
EC1R 0DA
Tel: 020 7812 3700
Website: www.drapersrecord.com

The fashion industry bible, this weekly publication is aimed at retailers and their suppliers and includes trends, news items, business articles and anything else concerned with fashion.

The Grocer
Broadfield Park
Brighton Road
Pease Pottage
Crawley
RH11 9RT
Tel: 01293 613400
Website: www.grocertoday.co.uk

This weekly publication has news and views about all
aspects of the grocery trade.

The Independent Retailer
Adam House
Waterworks Road
Worcester
WR1 3EZ
Tel: 01905 613106
Website: www.indretailer.co.uk

This is aimed at owners of independent retail outlet stores
throughout the UK and covers everything from c-shops to
garage forecourts. It is a monthly magazine.

Multiple Buyer & Retailer
448 St Davids Square
London
E14 3WH
Tel:020 7538 3973
Website: www.william-reed.co.uk

This monthly magazine is read by retail buyers and store
managers to get news on marketing, new products and
business issues.

Retail Therapy
(See under Skillsmart)

Retail Week
33–39 Bowling Green Lane
London
EC1R 0DA
Tel: 020 7505 8000

Aimed firmly at the large retail market this weekly magazine
has information on all aspects of retail.

Scottish Local Retailer (SLR)
2nd floor Waterloo Chambers
19 Waterloo Street
Glasgow
G2 6AY
Tel: 0141 222 2100

Covering the whole of Scotland SLR is a monthly magazine
including product launches, marketplace analysis and ideas
for retailers to improve their businesses.

ONLINE RESOURCES

InRetail
Website: www.inretail.co.uk

This is the leading recruitment website for the retail industry
in the UK. It contains retail news, gives very useful
descriptions of jobs within the industry, has a section
exclusively for graduates and also has a comprehensive list
of jobs you can apply for by email.

InterQuest
Website: www.interquest.co.uk

If your area of interest in retail lies within IT then you should check out this website. The InterQuest Group Ltd provides IT personnel across the retail sector including systems analysis, database administration and infrastructure support. It has a specialist candidate database for IT staff, either in permanent positions or interim staff for particular projects. More information is available from retail@interquest.co.uk

Meridian
Website: www.meridianretail.co.uk

A specialist retail recruitment consultancy, Meridian deals with retail multiples across the UK as well as European and American groups. Most of the appointments made through Meridian are in the shop floor or Head Office sectors of retail.

Retail Human Resources
Website: www.rhr.co.uk

This is the largest recruitment consultancy in the UK specialising in retail appointments. Retail Human Resources has 11 offices in the UK and handles vacancies in everything from buying, merchandising and distribution to human resources and technical & design.